Traditional Hymns

Complements All Piano Meth

T0040619

Table of Contents

Traditional Hymns Level 3 is designed for use with the third book of any piano method.

Concepts in *Level 3*:

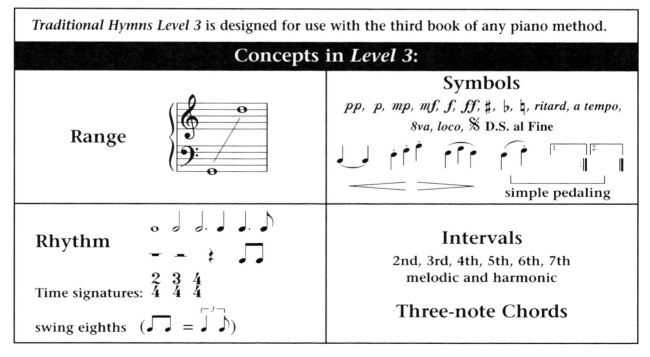

Range	Symbols
	pp, *p*, *mp*, *mf*, *f*, *ff*, ♯, ♭, ♮, *ritard*, *a tempo*, *8va*, *loco*, 𝄋 D.S. al Fine
	simple pedaling
Rhythm Time signatures: 2/4 3/4 4/4 swing eighths	Intervals 2nd, 3rd, 4th, 5th, 6th, 7th melodic and harmonic **Three-note Chords**

ISBN 0-634-03679-3

HAL•LEONARD®
CORPORATION

7777 W. BLUEMOUND RD. P.O. BOX 13819 MILWAUKEE, WI 53213

Visit Hal Leonard Online at
www.halleonard.com

Tell Me The Stories Of Jesus

Words by William H. Parker
Music by Frederic A. Challinor
Arranged by Fred Kern

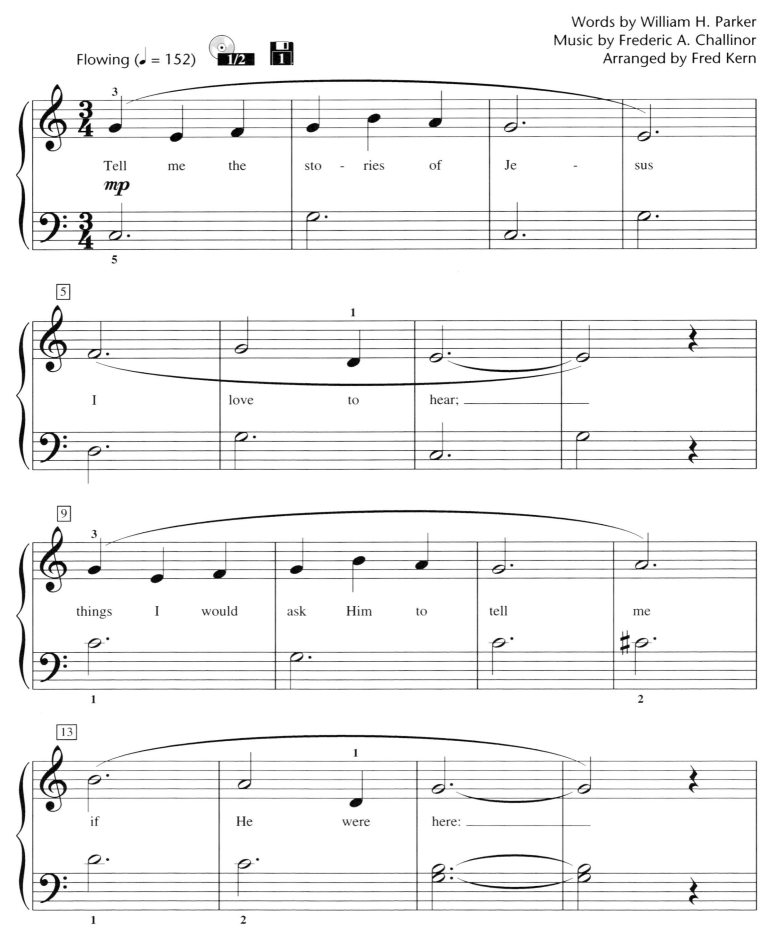

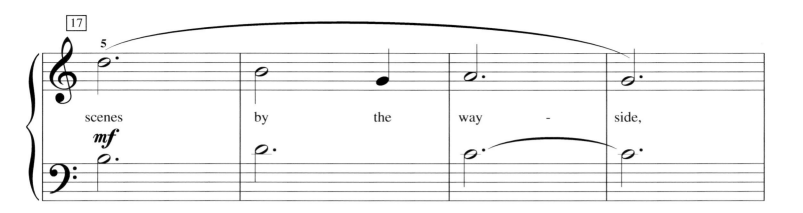

scenes　　　　by　　　　the　　　way - side,

mf

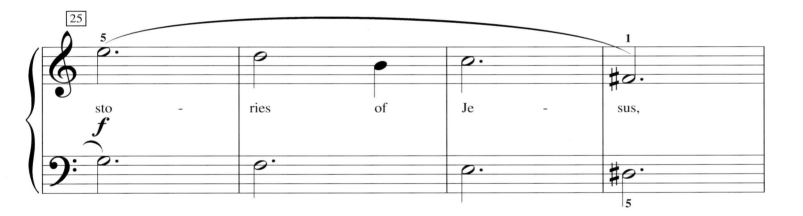

tales　　　　of　　　　the　　　sea,

cresc.

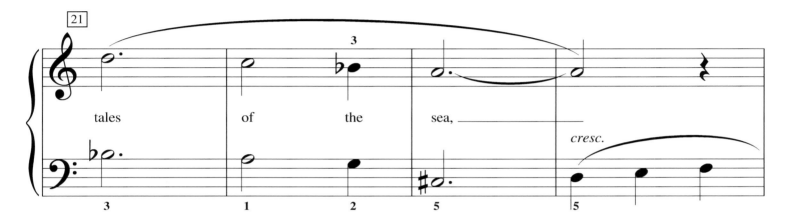

sto - ries　　　of　　　Je - sus,

f

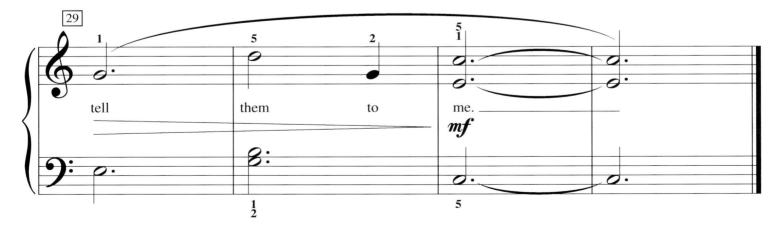

tell　　　them　　　to　　　me.

mf

From All That Dwell Below The Skies

Words by Isaac Watts
Music by John Hatton
Arranged by Phillip Keveren

With majesty (♩ = 112)

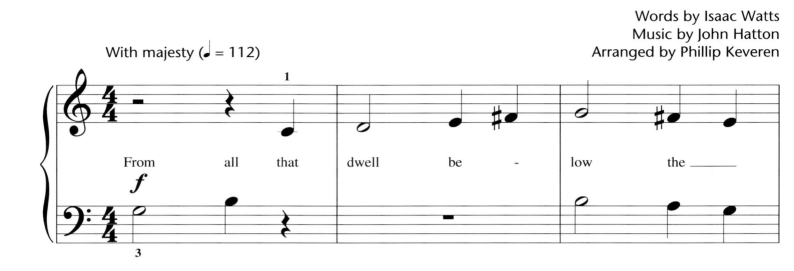

Accompaniment (Student plays one octave higher than written.)

With majesty (♩ = 112)

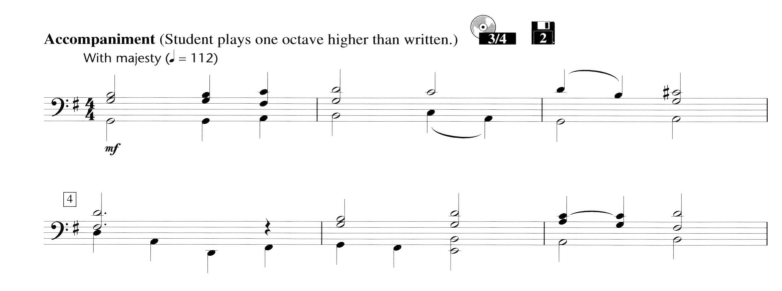

praise a - rise. Let the Re - deem - er's

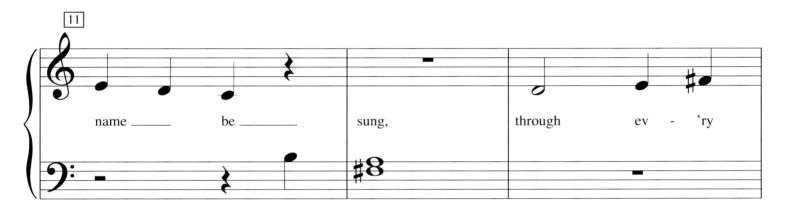

name _____ be _____ sung, through ev - 'ry

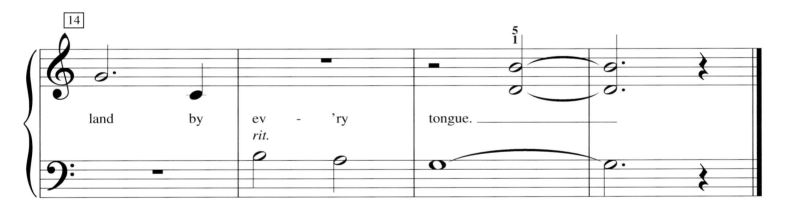

land by ev - 'ry tongue. _____

rit.

rit.

A Mighty Fortress Is Our God

Words and Music by Martin Luther
Translated by Frederick H. Hedge
Based on Psalm 46
Arranged by Fred Kern

Accompaniment (Student plays one octave higher than written.)

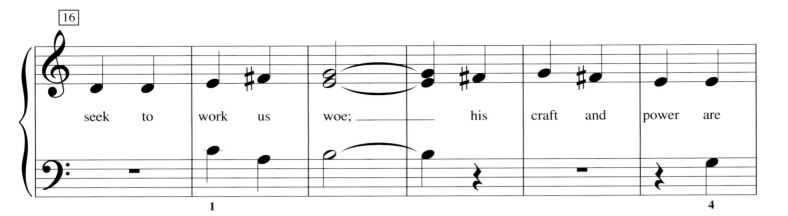

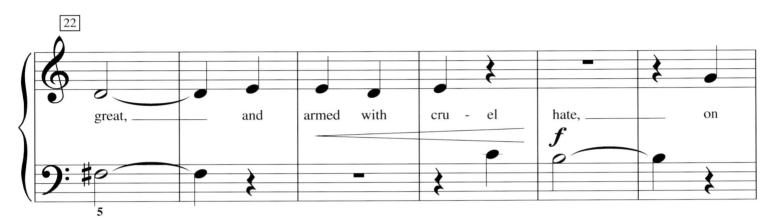

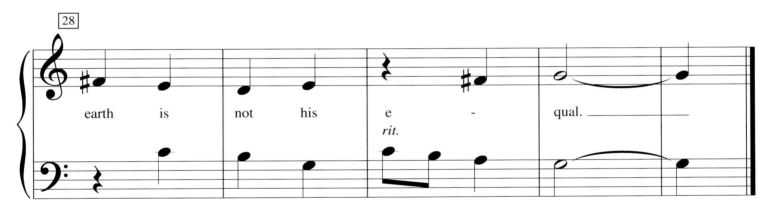

Come, Thou Almighty King

Traditional
Music by Felice de Giardini
Arranged by Fred Kern

Boldly (♩ = 112)

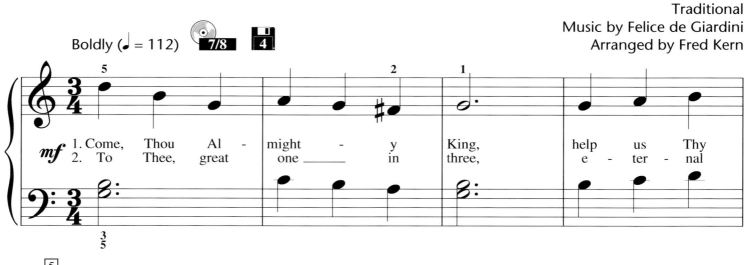

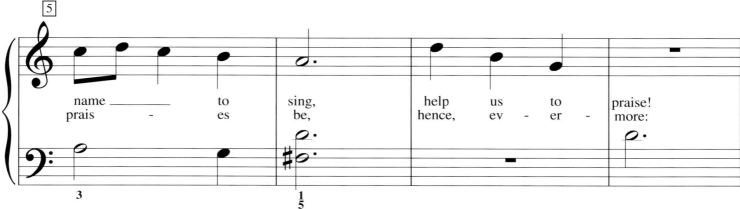

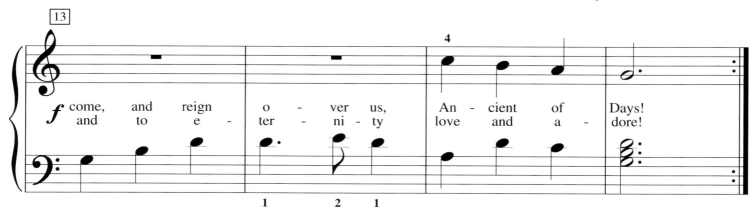

Jacob's Ladder

African-American Spiritual
Arranged by Fred Kern

Slowly, with feeling (♩ = 108)

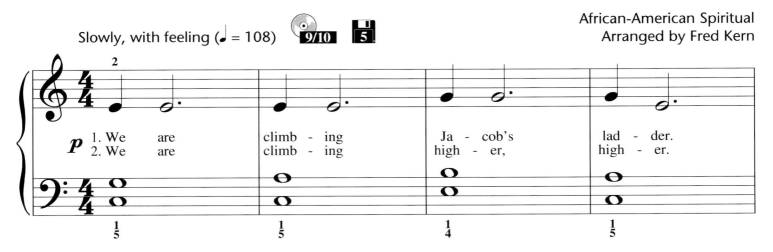

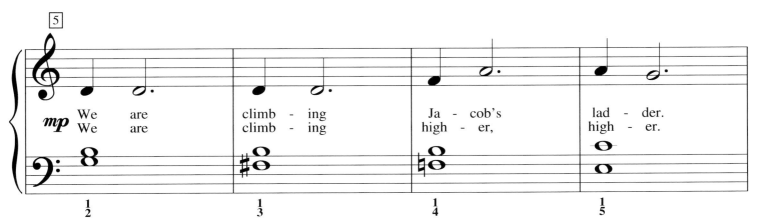

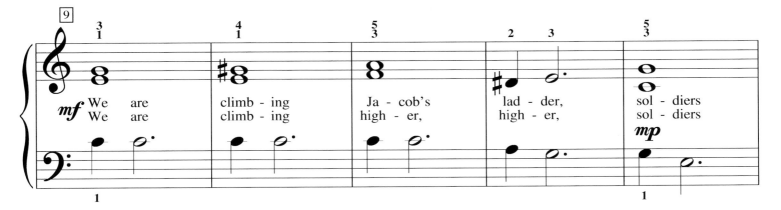

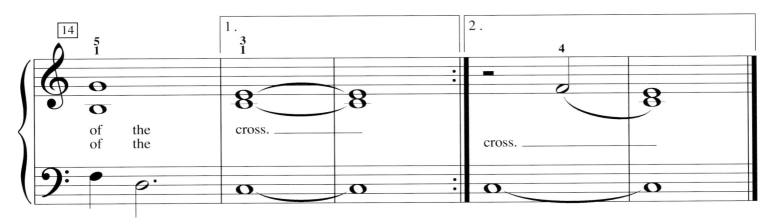

Zacchaeus

Traditional
Arranged by Mona Rejino

With spirit (♩ = 138)

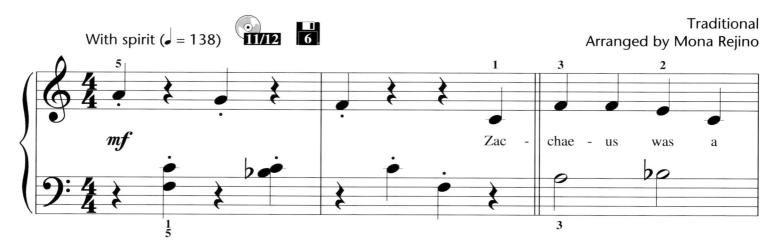

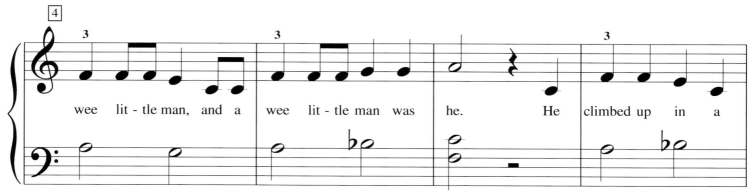

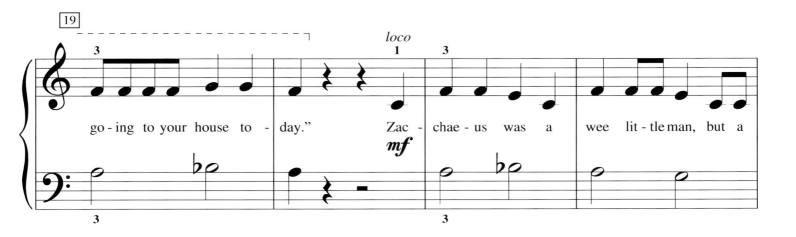

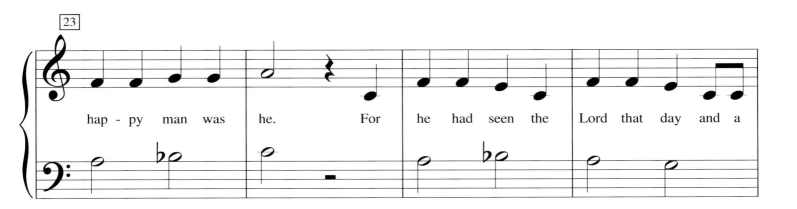

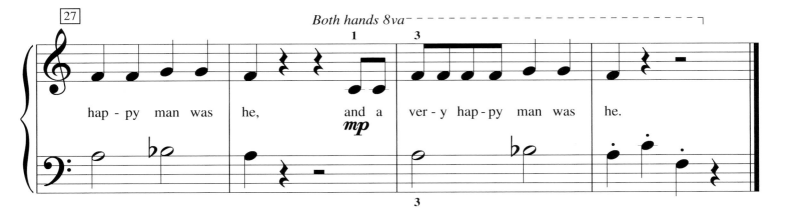

Lead On, O King Eternal

Words by Ernest W. Shurtleff
Music by Henry T. Smart
Arranged by Mona Rejino

Majestically (♩ = 100)

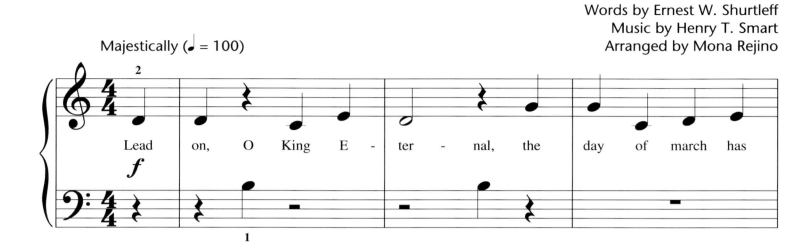

Lead on, O King E - ter - nal, the day of march has

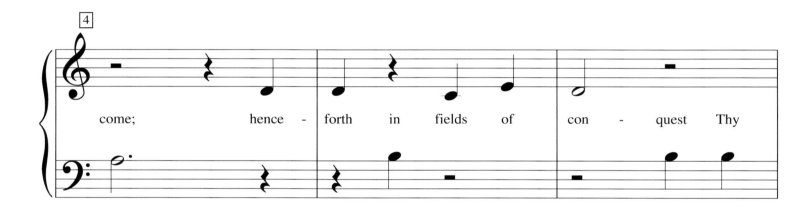

come; hence - forth in fields of con - quest Thy

Accompaniment (Student plays one octave higher than written.) **13/14** **7**

Majestically (♩ = 100)

tents shall be our home. Thro' days of prep - a -

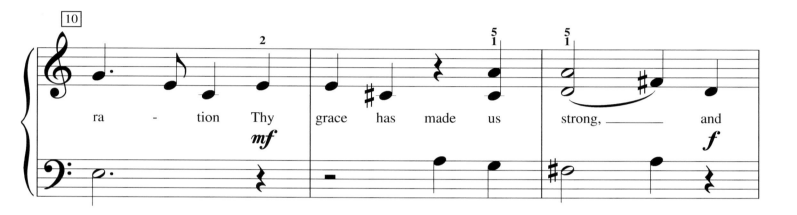

ra - tion Thy grace has made us strong, _____ and

now, O King E - ter - nal we lift our bat - tle song.

Dear Lord And Father Of Mankind

Words by John Greenleaf Whittier
Music by Frederick Charles Maker
Arranged by Mona Rejino

Holy, Holy, Holy! Lord God Almighty

Words by Reginald Heber
Music by John B. Dykes
Arranged by Mona Rejino

It Is Well With My Soul

Words by Horatio G. Spafford
Music by Philip P. Bliss
Arranged by Phillip Keveren

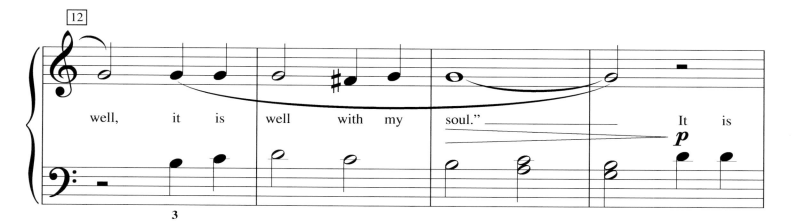

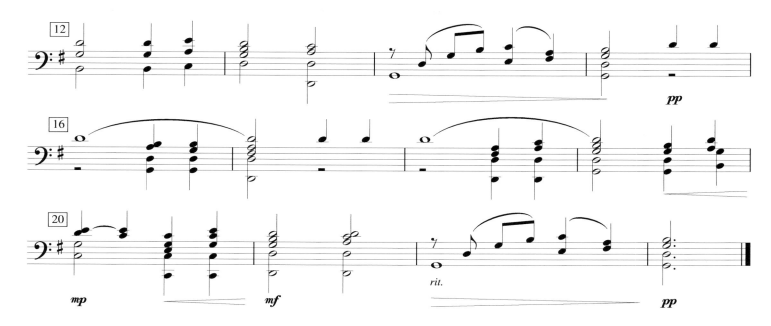

All Things Bright And Beautiful

Words by Cecil Frances Alexander
17th Century English Melody
Arranged by Martin Shaw
Arranged by Mona Rejino

made their glow - ing ___ col - ors, He ___ made their ti - ny ___

cresc.

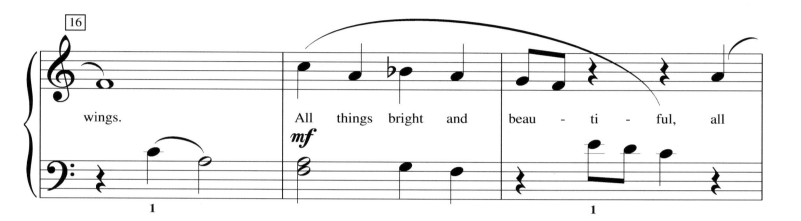

wings. All things bright and beau - ti - ful, all

mf

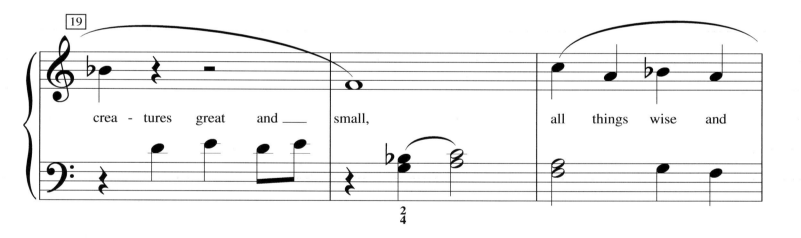

crea - tures great and ___ small, all things wise and

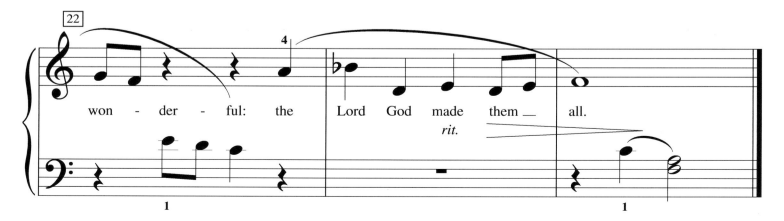

won - der - ful: the Lord God made them ___ all.

rit.

19

Little David, Play On Your Harp

Traditional
Arranged by Phillip Keveren

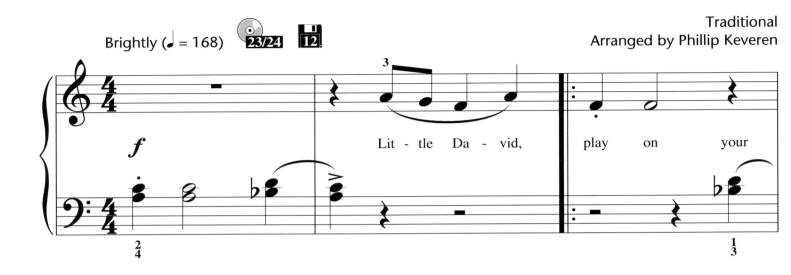

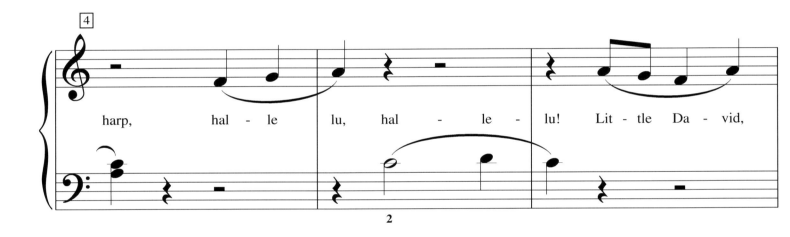

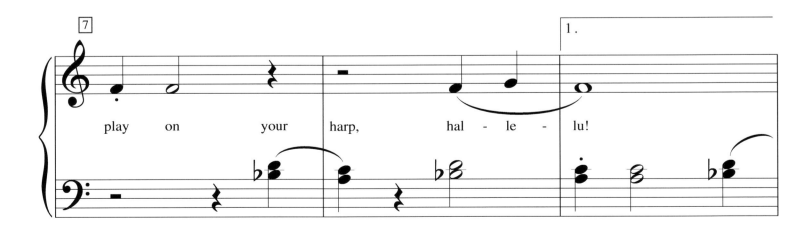

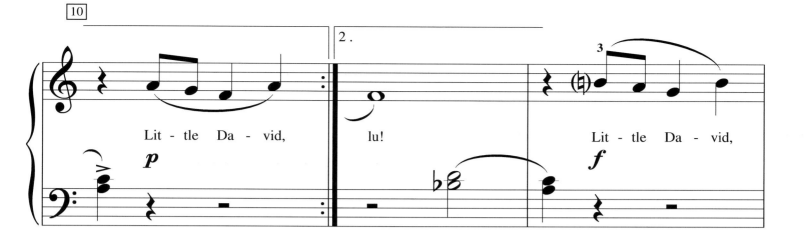

Lit - tle Da - vid, lu! Lit - tle Da - vid,

p   *f*

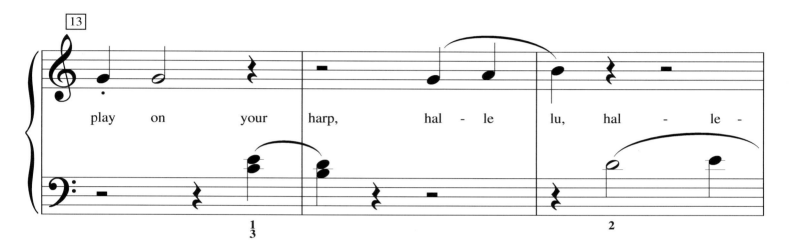

play on your harp, hal - le lu, hal - le -

lu! Lit - tle Da - vid, play on your harp, hal - le -

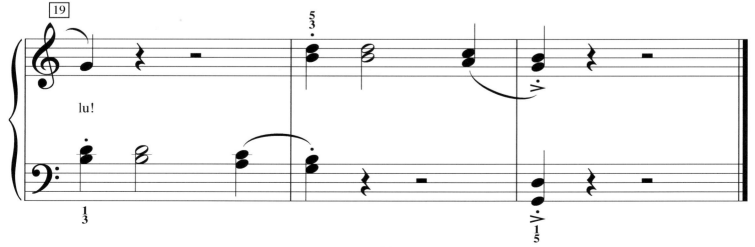

lu!

Ezekiel Saw The Wheel

Traditional Spiritual
Arranged by Phillip Keveren

Easy four (♩♩ = ♩ ♪) (♩ = 116)

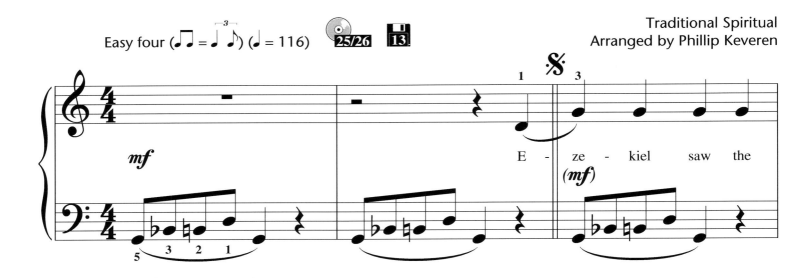

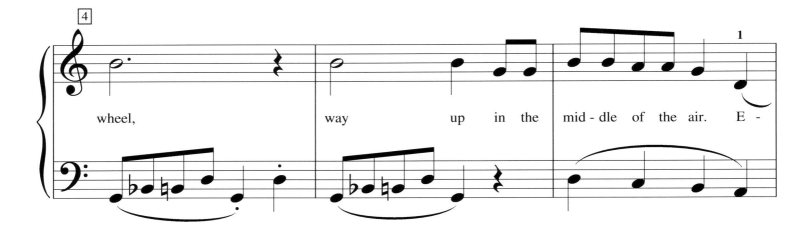

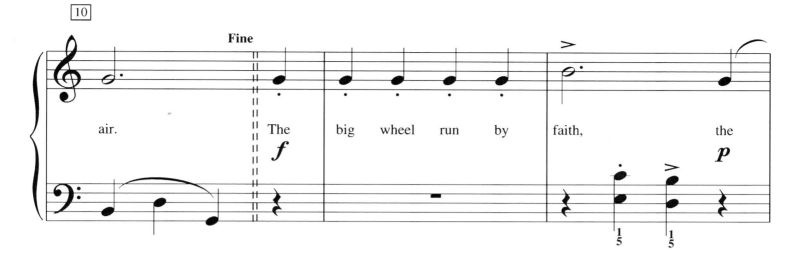

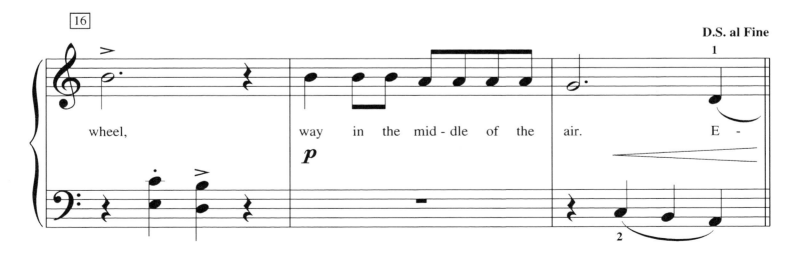

God Of Grace And God Of Glory

Words by Harry Emerson Fosdick
Music by John Hughes
Arranged by Fred Kern

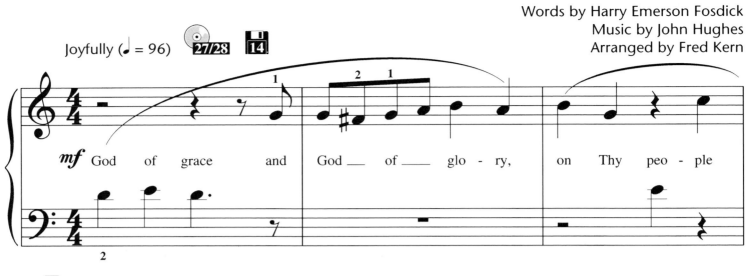

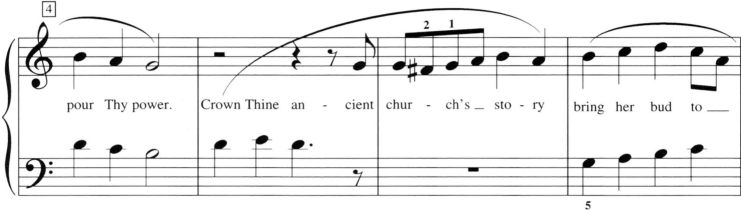

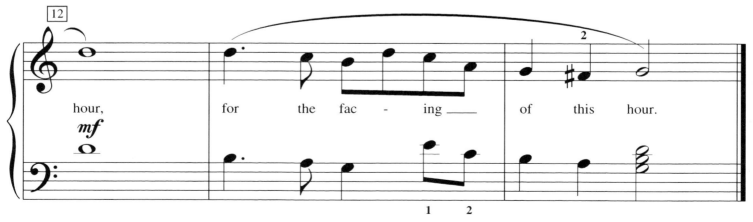